To Ted,

Love Mum,

xx.

First published 1998

ISBN 0 7110 2570 3

Published by

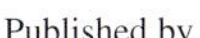

an imprint of Ian Allan Ltd, Terminal House, Station Approach, Shepperton, Surrey TW17 8AS.

Printed by Ian Allan Printing Ltd at its works at 'Riverdene', Hersham, Surrey KT12 4RG.

Code: 9705/

Front cover: Beyer Peacock 2-4-0T No 4 *Loch* (left) passes No 13 *Kissack* at Ballasalla on 1 July 1974. *C. M. Whitehouse*

Back cover: The classic lines of the Manx Beyer Peacock 2-4-0Ts are shown off to perfection as No 11 *Maitland* stands ready for duty at Douglas on 25 June 1960. *C. M. Whitehouse*

Title page: Ballagawne level crossing is located between Colby and Port St Mary. In the 1970s the keeper and friend are seen waving enthusiastically at the train. *John Hunt*

ISLE OF MAN STEAM RAILWAY

in colour

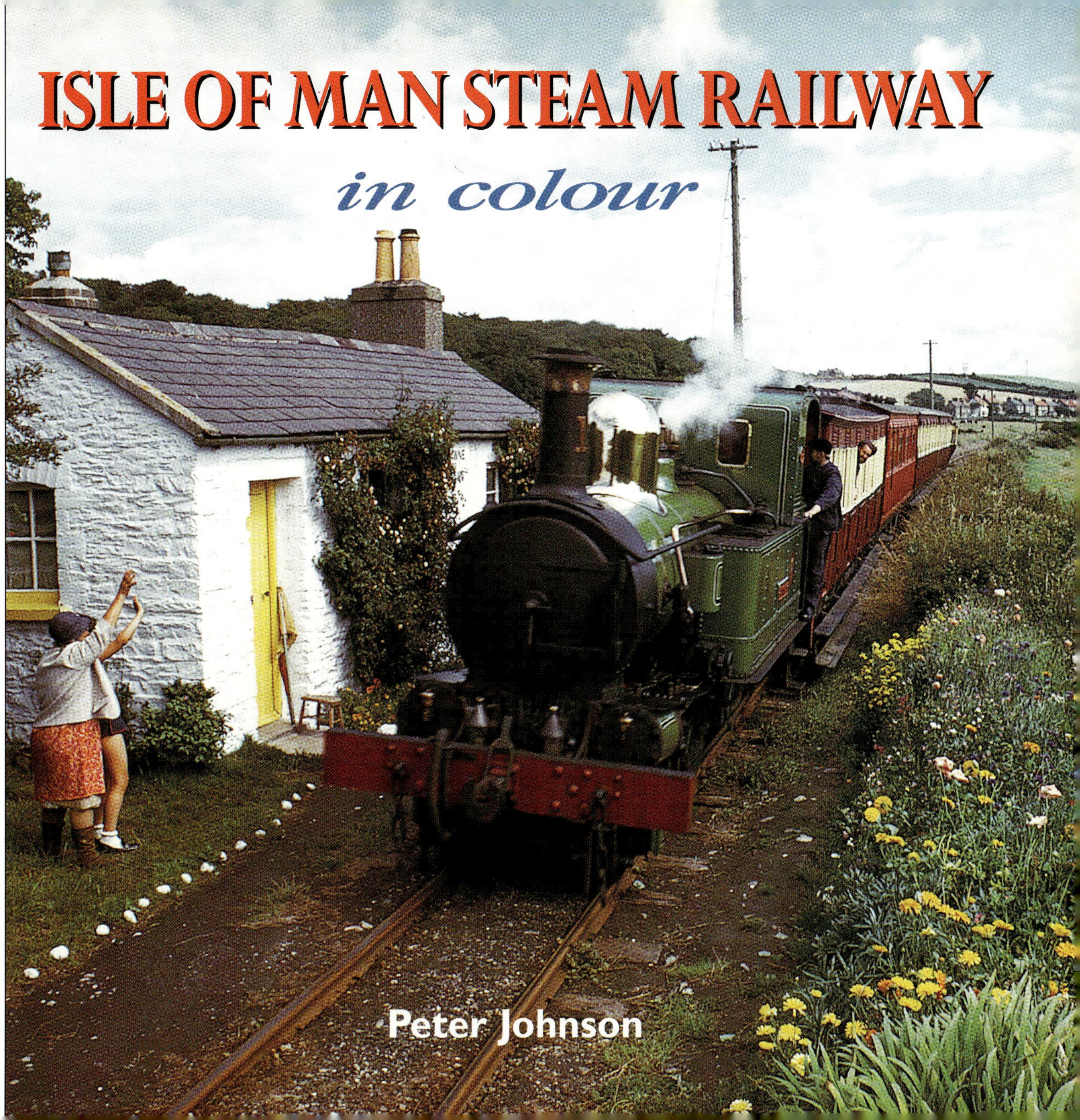

Peter Johnson

Introduction

For many railway enthusiasts a visit to the Isle of Man was, and is, a first trip away in the search for exotic steam action. Indeed, until the early 1970s the Isle of Man Railway Co was still a Victorian railway company, running a service with its origins in Victorian times and mostly with Victorian equipment. With the exception of the 1926-built locomotive No 16 *Mannin*, even locomotives and carriages obtained in the 20th century looked like their Victorian predecessors. The chances of the less knowledgeable being able to tell the difference were extremely unlikely. For the enthusiasts visiting the island during the last half century this was, and is, the big attraction.

It is indeed remarkable that these 50 years have actually seen more changes to the island's railways than at any time since their construction. Let us summarise briefly the Isle of Man Railway's history.

The Isle of Man Railway Co was incorporated on 19 December 1870. The initial objectives were to connect Douglas, Peel, Ramsey and Castletown by rail. A track gauge of 3ft was decided upon. Shortage of funds led the company to abandon the Ramsey proposal in 1872.

The railway between Douglas and Peel, 12 miles, was opened on 1 July 1873. Before construction began on the Castletown line, it was decided to extend it to Port Erin, giving a 15½-mile line that was opened on 1 August 1874.

The Manx Northern Railway was incorporated on 22 March 1877 to build and operate a 16-mile line, also 3ft gauge, between St John's and Ramsey. This was opened on 23 September 1879. The Foxdale Railway Co came within the ambit of the MNR. It was incorporated on 16 November 1882 to build a 2½-mile line from St John's to Foxdale; the line opened in 1886 and was operated by the MNR from the outset.

In 1905 the Manx Northern and Foxdale Railways were taken over by the Isle of Man Railway, the Foxdale company actually having been in liquidation since 1891.

Passenger services on the Foxdale line were actually the first to be withdrawn, when the minimal two trains a day service ceased after 16 May 1940, complete closure taking place in 1943. Occasional use was made of the branch thereafter to remove mine waste, the final operation, a works train, occurring on 26 January 1960.

After World War 2 the Isle of Man Railway experienced a boom in summertime holiday traffic until British holidaymakers discovered the delights of holidaying in consistently warmer climes. A peak of 1 million passengers annually was reached in 1956.

By the 1960s the railway was in terminal decline, with revenue falling and failing to produce sufficient funds to cover operating costs or to meet either adequate maintenance or renewals. Winter services on the Peel and Ramsey lines ceased from 1960 and 1961, and on 13 November 1965 complete closure took place.

No 8 *Fenella* shunting a train of cattle vans in 1949. The loco was still wearing the Brunswick green livery which was being superseded by Indian red at the time the photograph was taken. *R. A. H. Baxter*

The three lines were reopened on a seasonal basis on 3 June 1967, thanks to the intervention of Lord Ailsa, who took a lease on the system from the company. But by the end of 1968 the financial situation was no better and on 7 September the system closed again, apparently for good.

By this time the state of the railways and their contribution to the island's economy had become an item on the political agenda and it became clear that complete closure could not be allowed. The Isle of Man Tourist Board agreed to subsidise Lord Ailsa to operate the south (Port Erin) line, always the most successful of the island's railways, on a seasonal basis for a three-year period. With the railway now marketed as the Isle of Man Victorian Steam Railway, this era ended with the close of the 1971 season, when Ailsa pulled out completely. While he had lost considerable sums on his railway adventure, Lord Ailsa also laid the foundation for the future, by investing in new boilers for two of the steam locomotives.

For the next three years the railway company operated the Port Erin line, again with governmental financial support. During this period the high point of the 1974 Port Erin line centenary celebrations can be contrasted with the lows brought about by the lifting of the closed lines to Peel, Foxdale and Ramsey, and the disposal for scrap of some allegedly 'surplus' but historic rolling stock.

In 1974 the Manx Government agreed to support railway operation for a further five years, but only between Port Erin and Castletown, a policy which turned out to have a disastrous effect on passenger numbers. It only lasted for 1975 and 1976 because a new Government, elected in 1976, decided to nationalise the railway.

Under government control, railway operation returned to Douglas in 1977. During the following 20 years the Isle of Man Steam Railway (the 'Victorian' epithet was quickly lost) has continued to be supported by both Manx Government and visitors. Enough support comes from the latter, indeed, to encourage continued investment in the railway by the former. While resources are not limitless, and there have been some losses, both infrastructure and rolling stock have benefited since coming into Government ownership.

Not surprisingly, the steam locomotives attract most attention, for the newest currently operating dates from 1908. Of the 14 Beyer Peacock 2-4-0Ts owned by the old company, 11 still exist on the island, although not all in railway ownership. The Manx Northern Railway owned four locomotives; two survive, both on the island: the 15th Beyer Peacock 2-4-0T and the notable 'odd man out', Dübs 0-6-0T *Caledonia* of 1885, which spectacularly returned to steam with trips to the summit of Snaefell for the Snaefell Mountain Railway centenary in 1995.

Of particular interest in the year of publication of this book, coinciding with the 125th anniversary of the Peel line, is the return to service of No 1 *Sutherland*, one of the locomotives supplied for the opening of that route. After many years on display in the museum at Port Erin, it has been returned to Douglas for overhaul in time to participate in the 125th anniversary celebrations.

Around 30 years ago few would have forecast the continued existence of the railway with any confidence. That it is able to mark this anniversary with the appearance of a 'new' locomotive is all the more remarkable. Let us look forward with confidence to the 150th anniversary of the Isle of Man Steam Railway!

Peter Johnson
Leicester
January, 1998

peterjohnson@btinternet.com
http://www.btinternet.com/~peterjohnson/

Acknowledgements

Once more I am indebted to the photographers who have allowed me access to their collections. To Geoff Lumb and Michael Whitehouse (both again) and John Hunt I offer my sincere appreciation for the courtesy extended in supporting this project.

In their support for keeping the Port Erin line going the Manx people deserve every visitor's thanks, as do those who daily engage in the graft needed to run the trains. Without them there would be no book. The island of course has its own charms, among them the operators of its railways, many of them characters in their own right. The indefatigable Alan Corlett deserves particular mention for his role in masterminding the special events of the last five years and particularly in encouraging enthusiasts to return to the island, and its railways, again and again.

A full bibliography on the Isle of Man Railway would take more space than can be spared here but for comprehensive information about the railway and its history the inestimable James Boyd's *The Isle of Man Railway* (Oakwood Press, 3 vols, 1993-6) is recommended. Those who prefer their history briefer, and who perhaps have shallower pockets or lighter bookshelves, should try *The Isle of Man Steam Railway* by Barry Edwards (B&C Publications, 1996).

Douglas Scenes

Below: No 6 *Peveril* shunting carriages on 28 June 1956.
P. B. Whitehouse/C. M. Whitehouse Collection

Right: No 3 *Pender* shunts carriages while No 16 *Mannin* takes water. The railway's comprehensive goods facilities are in evidence on the right.
P. B. Whitehouse/C. M. Whitehouse Collection

Left: The loco crew relax while waiting for time with a Peel departure on 23 July 1968. The loco is No 11 *Maitland. P. B. Whitehouse/C. M. Whitehouse Collection*

Above: The 4.15pm Peel departure required more carriages, for it was the school train. No 6 *Peveril* was in charge on 28 June 1956.
P. B. Whitehouse/C. M. Whitehouse Collection

Above: With drain cocks open, No 12 *Hutchinson* leaves for Peel on 23 July 1968. No 11 *Maitland* stands behind. *C. M. Whitehouse*

Right: Nos 4 *Loch* and 11 *Maitland* double-head a special train in the autumn of 1977. *John Hunt*

Left: No 10 *G. H. Wood* sets off for Port Erin on 28 April 1995, with the County Donegal railcars standing outside the workshop. Built in 1950/1, the railcars were bought by the Isle of Man Railway in 1961. Initially used on passenger services, they were transferred to departmental use from 1975. Over subsequent years they became unfit for passenger service. Tenders have been invited for them to be overhauled and restored during the 1998/9 financial year. *Peter Johnson*

Right: Parallel departures seen from the steps of Douglas signal-box on 28 June 1956. *P. B. Whitehouse/ C. M. Whitehouse Collection*

Above: In October 1977 No 13 *Kissack* was photographed passing the railway's workshops. *Kissack* was built in 1910. Last used in 1991, its boiler was overhauled and transferred to No 10 *G. H. Wood* in 1993. Dutton and Co of Worcester installed the splendid signal gantry in 1892. *John Hunt*

Right: Nos 12 *Hutchinson* and 11 *Maitland* seen inside Douglas loco shed on 1 July 1974. *C. M. Whitehouse*

In the 1950s the railway still carried general goods as well as passengers. Regrettably, scenes such as this, showing some of the variety carried, rarely caught the attention of photographers.
P. B. Whitehouse/C. M. Whitehouse Collection

Locomotives

A busy scene outside Douglas loco shed on 25 June 1960. No 5 *Mona* is by the coal heap, No 12 *Hutchinson* is inside the loco shed and one of the former County Donegal Railway railcars is inside the workshop, while a third loco shunts two wagons loaded with coal. *P. B. Whitehouse/C. M. Whitehouse Collection*

No 1 *Sutherland* shunting at Douglas in the 1950s. The specification for the first engines required that they be capable of hauling 15 loaded four-wheel coaches up a gradient of 1 in 65. Built in 1873, No 1 was withdrawn with a defective boiler in 1964. In 1975 it became an exhibit in the Port Erin museum. At the time of writing it is being overhauled with No 8 *Fenella's* rebuilt boiler, to participate in 1998's 'Steam 125' events. *P. B. Whitehouse/C. M. Whitehouse Collection*

No 4 *Loch* shunting at Port Erin in May 1983. The worksplate painted onto the bunker was a feature of No 4 at this time. No 4 was built for the opening of the Port Erin line in 1874. *Peter Johnson*

No 6 *Peveril* by the Douglas coal pile on 28 June 1956. Built in 1875, No 6 was withdrawn from service in 1960. It was repainted for display purposes by volunteer supporters in 1994. *P. B. Whitehouse/C. M. Whitehouse Collection*

On 25 June 1960 No 10 *G. H. Wood* poses outside Douglas loco shed. No 10 was built in 1905; after a period out of use it was returned to traffic with No 13 *Kissack's* boiler in 1993. *P. B. Whitehouse/C. M. Whitehouse Collection*

Below: No 11 *Maitland*, built in 1905, receives attention during steam raising in May 1983. *Peter Johnson*

Right: A contrasting view of No 11 *Maitland* at Douglas on 19 July 1997. *Peter Johnson*

11
MAITLAND

Above: The contents of No 12 *Hutchinson's* smokebox under scrutiny during ash removal at Douglas on 23 July 1968. Built in 1908, No 12's cab was replaced with a 'square style' one in 1979. *P. B. Whitehouse/C. M. Whitehouse Collection*

Right: A veteran of 1910, No 13 *Kissack* is seen being prepared for another trip in August 1974. *John Hunt*

13
KISSACK
No13

Above: No 14 *Thornhill* was built for the Manx Northern Railway in 1880 as MNR No 3. Out of service since 1958, it was photographed at St John's on 23 July 1968. In 1978 it was sold for private preservation, and remains in secure storage on the island. *John Hunt*

Right: On 24 August 1952 former Manx Northern Railway No 4 *Caledonia*, Isle of Man Railway No 15, was caught at Douglas in this sombre black livery, with snowplough attached. *P. B. Whitehouse/C. M. Whitehouse Collection*

Far right: Caledonia was withdrawn in 1968 and put on display in Port Erin in 1975. In 1993 it was transferred to Douglas, where it was overhauled the following year. The photograph was taken on 25 July 1997. *Peter Johnson*

M. N. Ry
CALEDONIA
No 4.

Above: Stylish contrasts at Douglas on 23 July 1997. From the left are No 12 *Hutchinson*, No 16 *Mannin* (both with 'square' cabs) and traditionally-styled No 11 *Maitland*, the latter en route to Port Erin. New in 1926, No 16 was the last locomotive built for the Isle of Man Railway; retaining its original boiler it was withdrawn in 1964 and was displayed at Port Erin from 1975. In 1997 it was stored at Douglas while the museum was rebuilt. *Peter Johnson*

Right: Inside Douglas loco shed on 25 July 1994, Nos 10 *G. H. Wood* and 12 *Hutchinson*, still warm after the day's work. No 12's livery dates from its 1979 overhaul. *Peter Johnson*

Below: Locomotive line-ups are a popular feature of the evening photography sessions held during enthusiast events. Seen on 22 July 1997 are No 9 *Douglas* (with wooden smokebox door), No 6 *Peveril*, No 11 *Maitland*, No 15 *Caledonia* and No 10 *G. H. Wood. Peter Johnson*

Right: Nos 12 *Hutchinson*, 10 *G. H. Wood* and 15 *Caledonia* seen at Douglas after dark on 25 July 1996. *Peter Johnson*

TICKETS

Closed Lines

Left: Kirk Braddan, on the Peel line, had the distinction of opening only on Sunday mornings, serving worshippers at a nearby church. Special operating was required on the railway to cope with the crowds, as seen here with two trains in section. The former County Donegal Railway railcars wait to operate the 11.50am departure to Douglas, while behind them No 5 *Mona* will follow with the 12pm departure. The board affixed to No 5 denotes 'special to follow in opposite direction'. The date was 19 July 1964. *Geoff Lumb*

Below: St John's, the junction of the Isle of Man Railway with the Manx Northern Railway and the Foxdale branch, saw much activity when trains were joined or divided there. On 29 June 1956 No 8 *Fenella* pulls the Ramsey portion of a Douglas-Peel/Ramsey train into the station.
P. B. Whitehouse/C. M. Whitehouse Collection

Left: No 5 *Mona* takes water at St John's on 29 June 1956. Built in 1874, *Mona* remained in service until 1968. *P. B. Whitehouse/C. M. Whitehouse Collection*

Above: No 12 *Hutchinson* is shrouded in steam when crossing the County Donegal railcars at Crosby on 23 July 1968. *C. M. Whitehouse*

Above: Peel station on 3 July 1956, with No 6 *Peveril* waiting to leave for Douglas. *P. B. Whitehouse/C. M. Whitehouse Collection*

Right: No 5 *Mona* awaits departure from Peel on 25 July 1964, while the railway lorry is loaded under the awning. *Vic Nutton, courtesy Geoff Lumb*

Nº 5
HALT
THE CREEK

Left: On 23 July 1964 No 5 *Mona* heads away from St John's with a Ramsey train. The divergence to Peel is on the right. *Geoff Lumb*

Left: On the Manx Northern Railway there were two splendid viaducts: at Glen Mooar and Glen Wyllin. The latter is seen here, being crossed by No 8 *Fenella* and a typically short train on 30 June 1956. *P. B. Whitehouse/ C. M. Whitehouse Collection*

Right: No 5 *Mona* at Kirk Michael, Manx Northern Railway, on 25 July 1964. *Vic Nutton, courtesy Geoff Lumb*

SWAN
VESTAS
GENTLEMEN

M.56

Left: No 11 *Maitland* shunting at the Manx Northern Railway's Ramsey terminus. Few of the 'M' series wagons survive, although one has just (late 1997) been restored by the Isle of Man Steam Railway Supporters' Association. *C. M. Whitehouse Collection*

Below: No 3 *Pender* waits to leave Ramsey in the 1950s. The last of the 1873 locos, *Pender* was withdrawn in 1959 and sold in 1978. Sectioned to demonstrate the inner workings of a steam locomotive, it is an exhibit at the Manchester Museum of Science and Industry. The brake/3rd coach F20 was the first of a series built by Metropolitan in 1896 and appears fresh out of the paint shop when photographed. F69, behind, was formed of a pair of four-wheel carriage bodies mounted onto a bogie underframe in 1923. *C. M. Whitehouse Collection*

A Trip Along the South Line — Douglas to Port Erin

Left: Steam Railway engine crews don't seem to need much encouragement to make a spectacular departure, as seen with the last train for Port Erin on 12 April 1993. *Peter Johnson*

Above: No 12 *Hutchinson* passes Douglas workshops with an enthusiast runpast in May 1983. *Peter Johnson*

Below: No 11 *Maitland* is seen again, returning to Douglas with a photographers' demonstration works train on 25 July 1997. *Peter Johnson*

Right: Keristal, on the climb to Port Soderick, is the location of this view of No 12 *Hutchinson* on 25 July 1996. *Peter Johnson*

W

Left: Nos 4 *Loch* and 11 *Maitland* at Keristal in September 1977. The formation of the Douglas Head Marine Drive Tramway is seen on the cliff tops. *John Hunt*

Above: The livery of No 12 *Hutchinson* matches the colour of the sky at Keristal on 19 July 1997. The 'square' cab is scheduled to be replaced by a new one with a traditional outline. *Peter Johnson*

Above: Passing trains at Port Soderick on 25 July 1997. No 11 *Maitland* is hauling a photographers' special works train, while No 12 *Hutchinson* is on the passenger working. *Peter Johnson*

Right: No 10 *G. H. Wood* at Port Soderick on 23 July 1964. *Geoff Lumb*

PORT SODERICK

Left: No 11 *Maitland* arrives at Santon on 21 July 1997. *Peter Johnson*

Above: Santon station is known for its palm trees, one of which is seen in this view of No 13 *Kissack*, taken on 1 July 1974. *C. M. Whitehouse*

Left: Leaving Santon, framed by the road overbridge, is No 13 *Kissack*. The working is the 2.10pm from Douglas on 1 July 1974. *C. M. Whitehouse*

Right: Token exchange at Ballasalla on 19 July 1997. The locomotives are No 12 *Hutchinson* and No 10 *G. H. Wood*. This scene makes an interesting contrast with the 1974 view reproduced on the front cover. *Peter Johnson*

I. M. R.
THIRD

2

Left: At Ballasalla the locomotives of longer trains stand by the water tank, making a popular afternoon photo location. No 12 *Hutchinson* pulls away on 20 July 1997. *Peter Johnson*

Above: On 22 July 1997 No 15 *Caledonia* passes the Silver Burn river near Ballasalla. The driver is whistling for Ballasalla level crossing. *Peter Johnson*

F.25
GUARD

Left: No 10 *G. H. Wood* at Castletown on 3 July 1974. *C. M. Whitehouse*

Right: In 1975 Castletown was the terminus of a train service based at Port Erin. No 11 *Maitland* is seen there in the afternoon of 2 July that year, running round before returning to Port Erin. *Peter Johnson*

Above: Castletown station was rebuilt early in 1994. No 4 *Loch*, running chimney- first towards Douglas that year, arrives there on 28 July 1994. *Peter Johnson*

Left: No 11 *Maitland* is again seen at Castletown on 2 July 1975, framed by the now-demolished waiting shelter, while it waits to return to Port Erin. *Peter Johnson*

Right: No 15 *Caledonia* leaves Castletown on 22 July 1997. *Peter Johnson*

Left: Castletown's stationmaster takes the token from No 13 *Kissack* in the 1970s. *John Hunt*

Right: Like Santon, Colby is one of the railway's request stations. No 13 *Kissack* is seen arriving there in the 1970s. *Vic Nutton, courtesy Geoff Lumb*

SWAN
VESTAS
Nº13

F 49
GUARD

Left: Loco gossip, while No 12 *Hutchinson* and train grace Port Erin's bay platform on 1 July 1974. *C. M. Whitehouse*

Above: On 23 July 1968 No 5 *Mona* rests at Port Erin soon after arrival there. *C. M. Whitehouse*

No 16 *Mannin* stands outside Port Erin loco shed on 2 July 1956. After several years of using the former goods shed (right) the Port Erin based loco is to resume using the original loco shed during 1998.
P. B. Whitehouse/C. M. Whitehouse Collection

Away From Home

Above: In 1995 *Caledonia* participated in the Snaefell Mountain Railway centenary celebrations, operating on both the SMR and the Manx Electric Railway during the year. On 28 April 1995 it undertook a trial run on the mountain for the benefit of the Inspector of Manx Railways. *Peter Johnson*

Inset: After demonstrating steam operation on two electric lines, Isle of Man Railways just had to devise a way of demonstrating electric traction on the steam railway. On 3 December 1997 MER No 33, drawing power from a generator mounted on a flat wagon coupled behind it, is seen climbing out of Douglas on a demonstration run to Port Erin for members of the the railway press. The occasion was a prelude to the 125th anniversary of the Peel line being celebrated in 1998. *Peter Johnson*

Overleaf: The 1993 Manx Electric Railway centenary celebrations created world-wide interest in the Isle of Man and its railways. For many visitors the key to this was 'Steam on the MER'. No 4 *Loch* was stabled at Laxey electric car sheds and ran trips from Laxey to Dhoon Quarry, about three miles, hauling the MER Winter Saloon Trailers. This picture of the ensemble climbing up to Minorca was taken on 12 April 1993. *Peter Johnson*

THE MANX ELECTRIC RAILWAY Co. LTD.
THE MANX ELECTRIC RAILWAY Co. LTD.
4